The Progressive Movement 1900–1920
Efforts to Reform America's New Industrial Society ™

LABOR LEGISLATION

The Struggle to Gain Rights for America's Workforce

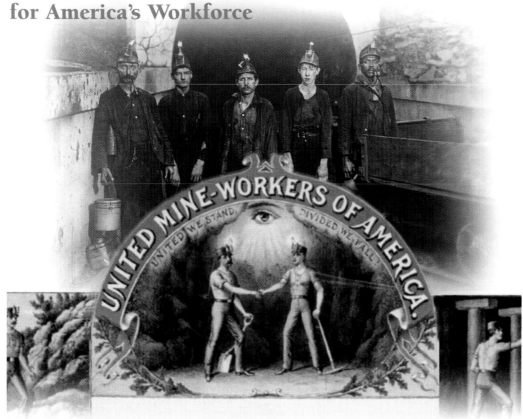

Katherine Lawrence

rosen central
Primary Source™

The Rosen Publishing Group, Inc., New York

For Christy Marx,
a fellow laborer in the field of writing and the best of best friends

Published in 2006 by The Rosen Publishing Group, Inc.
29 East 21st Street, New York, NY 10010

First Edition

Library of Congress Cataloging-in-Publication Data

Lawrence, Katherine, 1978–
Labor legislation : the struggle to gain rights for America's workforce / by Katherine Lawrence.
    v. cm.—(The progressive movement, 1900–1920: efforts to reform America's new industrial society)
Includes bibliographical references and index.
Contents: The Progressive Movement—Working in America—The government steps in— More laws, more improvements.
ISBN 1-4042-0191-2 (lib. bdg.)
ISBN 1-4042-0851-8 (pbk. bdg.)
6-pack ISBN 1-4042-6189-3
1. Labor laws and legislation—United States—History—20th century—Juvenile literature.
2. Progressivism (United States politics)—Juvenile literature. 3. United States—Economic conditions—1865–1918—Juvenile literature. [1. Labor laws and legislation. 2. Progressivism (United States politics) 3. United States—Economic conditions—1865–1918.]
I. Title. II. Series.
KF3319.6.L394 2004
344.7301'09'041—dc22
                                                                    2003028070

Manufactured in the United States of America

On the cover: Background image: Photograph of five coal miners in Gary, West Virginia, dated 1908. The other image is from a print called *United Mine-Workers of America*, date unknown.

Photo credits: Cover, pp. 5 (right), 7, 23 Library of Congress Prints and Photographs Division; p. 5 (left) © The Pierpont Morgan Library/Art Resource, N.Y.; p. 8 John Mitchell Papers/The American Catholic History Research Center and University Archives at the Catholic University of America; p. 11 courtesy David Rumsey Collection; pp. 13, 26 National Archives; p. 15 UNITE Archives, Kheel Center, Cornell University, Ithaca, N.Y.; pp. 17, 21 courtesy George Eastman House; p. 18 Library of Congress Manuscript Division; p. 19 © Corbis; p. 24 Minnesota Historical Society.

Designer: Les Kanturek; Editor: Annie Sommers; Photo Researcher: Amy Feinberg

Contents

Chapter One

The Progressive Movement

The years between 1900 and 1920 were a time of great change for the United States. The changes happened because people wanted things to be different. Before 1900, special interest groups, not voters, ruled the government. These groups—the very rich, corporations, and corrupt politicians—had the power to affect the government. This was something that was impossible for individuals to do. The groups could insist that state legislatures make their candidate a U.S. senator, because senators were decided by legislatures, not voters. They could propose new laws, such as reducing taxes, to make their lives easier.

However, many white, Protestant, well-educated men didn't like union members and immigrants having power. They believed these groups were changing the United States

"Hail to the King!"

John Pierpont Morgan *(right)* was born in 1837 and lived until 1913. He was very wealthy. Many people were not happy about this. The cartoon to the left is called "Hail to the King!" Drawn and written by a man named Allman, it shows Morgan as a king of the wealth in the United States. This cartoon is poking fun at how important and wealthy Morgan is.

in bad ways. They disliked the violence that happened when labor unions and business leaders couldn't agree. They didn't understand the religious beliefs of the many Catholic and Jewish immigrants. They wanted their own kind of America, an America where everyone was like them.

The only way to change things was to have a majority in Congress so they could pass new laws. This meant they had to win elections. To make voters like them, they called themselves Progressives. A vote against them was a vote against progress. They also said a vote for a Progressive candidate was a vote for the individual and not for a group such as a labor union.

It worked. In 1896, Republican William McKinley, a Progressive, was elected president of the United States. However, some politicians wanted to reform the government, not just for themselves but for everyone. This new kind of politician was called a Reformer.

One of the Reformers was Theodore Roosevelt. He spent most of his life in public service. He first served as a member of the New York State Assembly. Then, in 1898, he was elected governor of New York. He was so well respected that when President McKinley needed a vice president, the Republican Party offered the job to Roosevelt.

The team of McKinley-Roosevelt was elected in 1900, and the period of history called the Progressive movement began. Sadly, in September 1901, McKinley was assassinated. As a result, Theodore Roosevelt became the twenty-sixth president of the United States.

WE STAND FOR

The Gold Standard,

Protection and Prosperity,

Just Pension Laws,

And To Redeem All

REPUBLICAN PLEDGES

To The People.

FOR PRESIDENT
WILLIAM McKINLEY.

FOR VICE PRESIDENT
THEODORE ROOSEVELT.

This is a campaign poster for Republican presidential candidate William McKinley *(left)* and vice presidential candidate Theodore Roosevelt *(right)*. On September 6, 1901, McKinley was shot by a man named Leon Czolgosz in Buffalo, New York. He died eight days later. After McKinley was killed, Roosevelt became the youngest president at age forty-three.

Almost immediately, Roosevelt showed his desire for reform, starting with the relationship between workers and management. In 1902, the United Mine Workers quit working and went on strike in the coalfields of Pennsylvania. They wanted safer working conditions and higher pay. They also wanted management to acknowledge the existence of the United Mine Workers union. This would allow collective bargaining, in which a single union representative meets with management to negotiate for all union members.

The strike began in the summer. It was still going on in autumn when the weather turned cold. Schools and businesses closed because they had no coal for heating.

This is a photo of the United Mine Workers of America on strike in 1902. The official name of the strike was the Anthracite Coal Strike. It took place in Olyphant, Pennsylvania. The strike began after the coal operators refused to negotiate. It started on June 2, and as winter approached, people became very worried about the lack of coal.

That's when President Roosevelt stepped in. Earlier presidents had ended strikes by ordering everyone back to work. Roosevelt was different. He invited the leaders on both sides to the White House for a meeting. The miners agreed, but management refused. Roosevelt had to threaten to send federal troops to take over the mines before the company would negotiate.

Finally, an agreement was made. The mine workers got a pay increase in March 1903. Schools and businesses re-opened. However, the mine owners continued to refuse to give the United Mine Workers union any legal recognition.

How did relations between management and labor get so bad that the president had to threaten to send in the military? The cause can be found in the changes brought about by the Industrial Revolution.

Chapter Two

Working in America

The term "Industrial Revolution" refers to a time of great technological change that occurred in the United States between 1800 and 1900. During this period, new ways of making things were invented. Everything from clothing to building materials changed from being handmade to being manufactured by machines.

Before 1800, most people lived on farms and worked for themselves. After 1800, more and more people lived in cities and worked for others. Before the Industrial Revolution, business owners supervised a few workers who created things by hand. After the Industrial Revolution, they supervised hundreds of people who used machines to manufacture things.

Like everyone else, these business owners wanted to make as much money as possible. To do this, they had to keep their costs low. They paid workers as little as they

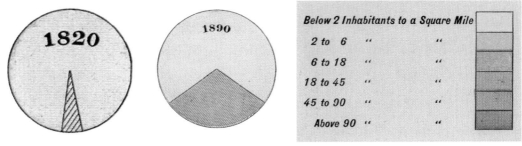

This colored map shows the population density of the United States in 1890. Population density refers to the number of people who live in a certain area. On the density legend *(far right)*, the most darkly shaded areas indicate where more than ninety people live per square mile. The two pie charts *(far left)* show that in 1820, a very small percentage of people lived in cities, as shown by the shaded area. In contrast, in 1890, there were more people in cities.

could. Why did workers put up with this? Why didn't they quit and go somewhere else? Because they had little choice. They worked because they needed to survive.

Without the money earned by working in the factories, workers couldn't buy food. They couldn't pay rent to keep a roof over their head. They couldn't buy coal to heat their homes in winter. Without these jobs, no matter how dreadful they often were, workers and their families would be homeless. They could starve to death or die from the cold in winter.

Workers did not have paid holidays or vacations. They didn't have sick days, where they got paid when they were sick and couldn't come to work. If a worker wasn't on the job working, he or she didn't get paid. If a worker was injured, it was up to the worker to pay all doctor and hospital bills. If a worker died, the business owner hired someone new. There was no payment to the family to make up for the loss of the worker's income.

The new factories also made workers obey rules. At many factories, everyone had to show up for work at the same time. All workers had to work the same hours. Also, workers were only allowed to take specified breaks. This meant that if a person wanted or needed a break, it was not possible. Unless, of course, the break

This photograph by Lewis Hine shows workers at a steel mill in Pittsburgh, Pennsylvania, in 1909. Hine had been hired by the National Child Labor Committee in 1908 to take photos of child laborers. Because of his photos, the public became aware of the terrible working conditions children faced. Slowly, laws were put in place to protect young workers and give them rights.

was in the specific time that had been chosen by the bosses. The day began at six o'clock in the morning and didn't end until six o'clock in the evening or later. That's a twelve-hour workday. They did this six days a week, Monday through Saturday.

Disaster Strikes

One of the most horrific workplace accidents happened on Saturday, March 25, 1911, in New York City. There were 500 workers, mostly young women, at the Triangle Shirtwaist Factory, which made shirts. Some of the women were girls, only fifteen years old. Late that afternoon, a fire started on the eighth floor of the factory. No one knows how it happened. It spread very quickly, and there was no escape for 146 of the 500 employees. Some jumped from the windows to their death. The rest died in the fire.

If a worker was late, he or she was fined. If a worker talked back to his or her supervisor, the worker was fined. There were rules for everything. And these were all meant to keep the worker on the job all day long.

There were accidents, sometimes deadly ones. Workers got caught in heavy machinery. Workers in the steel mills, which made rails for the new train routes, were often hurt or even killed in accidents with hot steel.

As a result of unsafe conditions and low wages, workers joined together, forming groups called labor unions.

After the horrible tragedy at the Triangle Shirtwaist Factory in New York City, many people got together to mourn those who had died. This photo shows people who had gathered together in an attempt to demand that progress be made in terms of giving workers more protection. A shirtwaist is a blouse with buttons down the front.

They believed that if all the workers in a factory refused to do their jobs, then management would have to improve conditions and increase wages. However, it didn't work that way.

Chapter Three

The Government Steps In

Between 1881 and 1897, U.S. workers went on strike more than 18,000 times. They hoped to force business owners to pay higher wages. They also wanted a shorter workday and wanted management to accept the unions.

However, business owners knew there were always people who had to work. More than twenty million immigrants arrived in the United States between 1871 and 1911. These new arrivals were desperate to find work so they could feed their families. Others needed money to pay the boat fare for family members to join them in America. Low pay, dangerous working conditions, long hours—none of it mattered as long as they were earning money.

Some states saw that workers needed help and tried to fix things. In 1893, Illinois passed a law called the Illinois Factory Act. This law limited the hours women could work in factories to eight a day. This meant they would only have to work a total of forty-eight hours a week. Sadly, two years later, the Illinois Supreme Court declared the law unconstitutional.

To be unconstitutional, the courts had to decide that the new law went against the U.S. Constitution. In this case, the court said that since the new law applied only to women who worked in factories and not those who worked in other locations, it was unfair to factory owners. Therefore, under the Constitution, it was not a valid law. The law was revoked, tossed out as if it had never existed.

Many immigrants who arrived in New York ended up at Ellis Island. This photo by Lewis Hine shows an Italian family who are looking for lost baggage after their long journey across the ocean. For a single mother with three children, this new life was going to be extremely difficult.

That same year, 1877, Massachusetts was the first state to pass a factory safety and health law. Other states soon followed. By 1897, there were fourteen states with factory safety laws.

This is the seal of the National Women's Trade Union League. Designed by Julia Bracken Wendt, the seal shows a woman in armor taking the hand of a mother with a child. Some of the rights the league wanted were an eight-hour workday and minimum wage.

The business owners weren't happy. Whenever possible, they suggested that the courts declare the new laws unconstitutional. It happened in state after state. The only solution was for the federal government to step in. Very little changed, however, until 1901, when Theodore Roosevelt became president.

Roosevelt believed big business should act fairly. When they didn't, he was happy to make laws to force them to do so. He wasn't the first, however. In 1887, President Grover Cleveland signed the Interstate Commerce Act. This act was the first time the U.S. government declared it had the power to regulate private business.

Before the Interstate Commerce Act, each railroad set its own prices for every customer, route, and item shipped. It was like a city bus charging a different price for each passenger on the bus. The act required everyone

This is a label from a medicine that is supposed to cure headaches, sore throats, sprains, bruises, cramps, toothaches, sore backs, and diarrhea—among other things. Hamlin's Wizard Oil was sold and marketed to help those who suffered from rheumatism (aches and pains). However, none of the ingredients in the Wizard Oil had to be listed. This meant that those who used the medicine never really knew for sure what they were taking!

on a route to pay the same amount for traveling or shipping.

In 1903, Roosevelt persuaded Congress to create a new department, the Department of Commerce and Labor. However, the federal government is only allowed to make rules for businesses that move products across state lines. If a company making lightbulbs sells those lightbulbs only in the same state where it manufactures them, then federal law doesn't affect it. This is because states have legal rights according to the Tenth Amendment to the U.S. Constitution.

The next department added to the government was the Food and Drug Administration (FDA). It was created as part of the 1906 Pure Food and Drug Act. At that time, many medicines contained addictive drugs like opium or cocaine. But there were no rules requiring an accurate list of ingredients. This act changed this potentially dangerous situation.

That same year, in his book *The Jungle*, Upton Sinclair wrote about the slaughterhouses and meat processing plants of Chicago. Those who read the book were disgusted by Sinclair's descriptions of the working conditions. They were even more shocked to learn that their sausages and hamburger contained anything that fell onto the factory floor. After this, the Meat Inspection Act was quickly passed.

The act established cleanliness standards for slaughterhouses and meat processing plants. Working conditions improved. In addition, all animals were required to pass inspection, both before and after processing. This ensured that only healthy animals became food.

President Roosevelt didn't stop his reforms with these acts. In 1908, he encouraged Congress to pass the Federal Employers' Liability Act. This law gave railroad workers and their families the right to ask for compensation (money) if a worker was injured or killed in a railroad-related accident. However, the act applied only to railroads that ran across state lines or handled interstate freight.

This was followed by the Sixteenth Amendment to the U.S. Constitution. Though proposed in 1909, the amendment was not ratified until 1913. The amendment gave Congress the power to tax "incomes, from whatever source" they came from. This was the first time there was a federal income tax. As a result, the government had money to spend as it chose, including to help workers.

Many serious workplace accidents took place before child labor laws came into effect. The victims were kids who were far too young to be operating heavy machinery and working long hours. This photo is by Lewis Hine. This young boy lost his arm while running a saw.

Chapter Four

More Laws, More Improvements

William Howard Taft became president in 1909. He was followed by Woodrow Wilson in 1913. He continued the reforms Roosevelt had begun. In 1916, Wilson signed the first nationwide law created to limit the use of child labor in mines and factories. The Keating-Owen Act made it illegal to sell items produced by children across state lines. Two years later, the Supreme Court declared the law unconstitutional.

Railroad workers were the targets of another law. The Adamson Act was passed in September 1916. This act set a standard eight-hour workday for railroad employees working for railroads that ran across state lines or handled interstate freight. It also required overtime pay at time and a half. This means each worker received 150 percent of the normal hourly wage for each hour worked beyond forty-eight hours in a six-day week.

"Mr. President, we don't want anything. We just want to grow up."

This political cartoon shows a crowd of child laborers. They are begging President Wilson to let them grow up. The cartoonist may be making a comparison to children who line up to see Santa and ask for presents for Christmas. These children just want to have safer working conditions so that they will not be killed or crippled on the job.

It wasn't until 1938, after the end of the Progressive movement, that the next labor law was passed. The Fair Labor Standards Act of 1938 set the first national minimum wage at $0.25 an hour. Until this time, each state or city could set its own minimum wage to be paid to workers. The act limited the maximum number of hours worked in a week to forty-four hours. This meant working Monday

A group of railroad workers are seen laying ties on the Minneapolis and St. Louis Railroad. In the cold, wintry months of 1887, these workers had to endure tough conditions as they worked tirelessly outdoors.

through Friday with a half-day on Saturday. If additional hours were worked in a week, companies had to pay time and a half for overtime.

The following year, the act raised the minimum wage to $0.30 an hour. As well, the maximum number of hours that was to be worked was reduced to forty-two hours. In 1940, the maximum number of hours that had to be worked was changed to forty each week.

Like other federal laws, the Fair Labor Standards Act didn't apply to everyone. It affected only those working for businesses involved in the production of goods transported across state lines. This included everything from screwdrivers to racehorses.

In 1942, the Fair Labor Standards Act was modified. The workweek was shortened to forty hours. The five-day workweek followed by a two-day weekend was required for all affected businesses.

Minimum wage has continued to grow over the years. At the end of 2003, it was officially no less than $5.15 an hour according to the Fair Labor Standards Act. (Some cities and states have a higher minimum wage.) Overtime pay of at least one and one-half times the regular rate of pay is required after forty hours of work in a workweek. Considering that 100 years ago, no

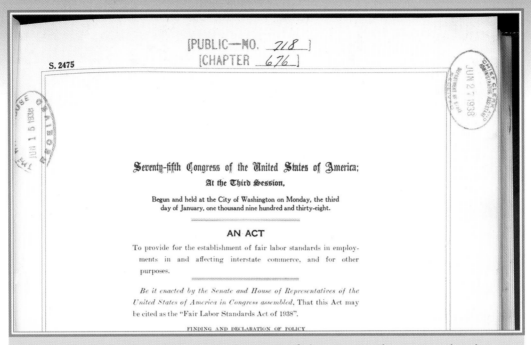

Seventy-fifth Congress of the United States of America;

At the Third Session,

Begun and held at the City of Washington on Monday, the third
day of January, one thousand nine hundred and thirty-eight.

AN ACT

To provide for the establishment of fair labor standards in employ-
ments in and affecting interstate commerce, and for other
purposes.

*Be it enacted by the Senate and House of Representatives of the
United States of America in Congress assembled,* That this Act may
be cited as the "Fair Labor Standards Act of 1938".

FINDING AND DECLARATION OF POLICY

This is an excerpt of an actual page of the Fair Labor Standards Act of 1938. The act was signed on June 25, 1938. The Seventy-fifth Congress met to discuss it on Monday, January 3, in Washington, D.C. This was but the beginning of creating a safer, cleaner, and more just workplace for workers.

such thing as a minimum wage existed, things have definitely improved.

While the men who started the Progressive movement may have been selfish in their reasons, the end result has been of benefit to almost everyone. The American workplace is a safer place now than it has been at any time in U.S. history.

assassinated (uh-SA-sin-ayt-ed) Murdered by sudden or secret attack.

candidate (KAN-dih-dayt) Someone who seeks or is nominated for a political office.

collective bargaining (kuh-LEK-tiv BAR-gen-ing) Negotiation of wages and/or benefits between an employer and an organized group of employees.

commerce (KAH-mers) The buying or selling of merchandise.

compensation (kom-pen-SAY-shun) Money paid to make up for an injury or loss.

Congress (KON-gres) The national legislative body of the United States. It is made up of the House of Representatives and the Senate.

Constitution (kon-stih-TOO-shun) The body of written rules and laws by which the United States is governed.

freight (FRAYT) Goods in containers transported by water, air, or land; cargo.

interstate (IN-ter-stayt) Connecting or existing between two or more states.

labor union (LAY-ber YOON-yun) A group of workers united by common work-related interests for the purpose of collective bargaining.

legislature (LEH-jis-lay-chur) A body of people having the power to make laws.

middle class (MIH-dul KLAS) A class of society between an upper and lower class. It includes professionals and business workers.

negotiate (nih-GOH-shee-ayt) To discuss with another so as to arrive at the settlement of a matter.

overtime (OH-ver-tym) Time in excess of a standard day or week. Currently, this refers to any time worked after eight hours in a day or forty hours in a week.

profit (PRAH-fit) The amount of income a company or business keeps after deducting the cost of wages, raw materials, and other expenses.

Progressive (pruh-GREH-siv) Encouraging and supporting political or social progress and reform.

Protestant (PRAH-tes-tunt) A Christian not of the Catholic or Orthodox Church. A member or follower of any of the Christian churches derived from the Reformation.

ratify (RA-tih-fy) To approve or confirm.

reform (rih-FORM) To change or improve.

representative (reh-prih-ZEN-tuh-tiv) A person chosen to speak for others.

senator (SEH-nuh-ter) A member of a governing body, especially the United States Senate.

slaughterhouse (SLAH-tur-hows) A place or building where animals are killed and then their meat is turned into food.

Supreme Court (suh-PREEM KORT) The highest court in the United States. There are nine justices who sit on the Court and make decisions relating to the U.S. Constitution.

unconstitutional (un-kon-stih-TOO-shuh-nul) Violating the laws of the United States as written in the U.S. Constitution and Bill of Rights.

wage (WAYJ) A payment for labor or services.

Web Sites

Due to the changing nature of Internet links, the Rosen Publishing Group, Inc., has developed an online list of Web sites related to the subject of this book. This site is updated regularly. Please use this link to access the list:

http://www.rosenlinks.com/pmnhnt/lale

Primary Source Image List

Cover images: (Background) A Lewis Hine photo of five miners at the entrance to a coal mine, Gary, West Virginia. Dated September 1908. From the Library of Congress Prints and Photographs Division, Washington, D.C. The other three images are from an undated print entitled *United Mine-Workers of America*, also from the Library of Congress.

Page 5 (right): Portrait of John Pierpont Morgan, dated circa 1902. From the Library of Congress.

Page 5 (left): A cartoon called "Hail to the King!" by Allman. Printed in the *Toledo News-Bee* on January 5, 1910. Archived in the Pierpont Morgan Library.

Page 7: Campaign poster for William McKinley and Theodore Roosevelt circa 1900. This lithograph is housed at the Library of Congress.

Page 8: A photo of the United Mine Workers of America in Olyphant, Pennsylvania, in 1902. This is part of the John Mitchell Collection.

Page 11: Map, pie charts, and population density legend for 1890 from Rand McNally Company in 1897. From the David Rumsey Collection.

Page 13: A Lewis Hine photograph called "In the Mill," dated 1909, Pittsburgh, Pennsylvania. From the National Archives and Records Administration, Records of the Work Projects Administration.

Page 15: A photo of mourners and protesters after the Triangle Shirtwaist Factory fire of 1911. Image from the Kheel Center for Labor-Management Documentation and Archives at Cornell University.

Page 17: A Lewis Hine photo of an Italian immigrant family arriving at Ellis Island in 1905. Part of the Lewis Hine Memorial collection from the George Eastman House.

Page 18: Pen-and-ink drawing of the seal of the National Women's Trade Union League, circa 1903. Created by Julia Bracken Wendt. Housed at the Library of Congress.

Page 19: A lithograph of the label of Hamlin's Wizard Oil. Created by Hughes Litho. Co. in 1889.

Page 21: A Lewis Hine portrait of an injured child laborer from 1909. It's from a series of photos called Child Labor (Factories) series. Part of the Lewis Hine Memorial collection from the George Eastman House.
Page 23: An illustration from *Life* magazine. Published on June 19, 1913. Housed at the Library of Congress.
Page 24: A photo by H. G. Klenze of railroad workers laying railroad ties for the Minneapolis and St. Louis Railroad. Dated circa 1887. From the Minnesota Historical Society.
Page 26: An excerpt from the Fair Labor Standards Act of 1938. From the National Archives and Records Administration. It was signed on June 25, 1938.

Index

About the Author

Katherine Lawrence has had more than thirty television scripts produced, most recently for *Stargate Infinity*. She was nominated for a Writers Guild of America Award in 1997 for her "Ice Bound" episode of the ABC series *Hypernauts*. Other credits include writing computer games, short stories, a book on actor/martial artist Jean-Claude Van Damme, and a biography on children's book author Laurence Yep. She lives in the Sonoran Desert of Arizona. Please visit her Web site at http:// www.katherinelawrence.com.